MADE IN MICHIGAN WRITERS SERIES

General Editors

Michael Delp, Interlochen Center for the Arts

M. L. Liebler, Wayne State University

Advisory Editors

Melba Joyce Boyd

Wayne State University

Stuart Dybek

Western Michigan University

Kathleen Glynn

Jerry Herron

Western Michigan University

Laura Kasischke

University of Michigan

Frank Rashid

Marygrove College

Doug Stanton

Author of *In Harm's Way*

*A complete listing of the books in this series
can be found online at wsupress.wayne.edu*

After-Music

POEMS BY CONRAD HILBERRY

WAYNE STATE UNIVERSITY PRESS

DETROIT

12 11 10 09 08   5 4 3 2 1

Library of Congress Cataloging-in-Publication Data

Hilberry, Conrad.
  After-music : poems / by Conrad Hilberry.
    p. cm. — (Made in Michigan writers series)
  ISBN-13: 978-0-8143-3352-5 (pbk. : alk. paper)
  ISBN-10: 0-8143-3352-4 (pbk. : alk. paper)
  I. Title.
  PS3558.I384A69 2008
  811'.54—dc22
  2007024010

mc aca michigan council for arts and cultural affairs

This book is supported by the Michigan Council for Arts and Cultural Affairs

Grateful acknowledgment is made to the DeRoy Testamentary Foundation for the support of the Made in Michigan Writers Series.

∞

Designed by The DesignWorks Group
Typeset by Maya Rhodes
Composed in Mrs Eaves, Bee Three T, and Jefferson

For Marion, Marilyn, Jane, and Ann

CONTENTS

ONE Sweet Grease

MARIO

How did he get in Portuguese 202?

He's from Brazil, he *speaks* Portuguese—

a Brazilian kind of Portuguese, folding in

some rainy toucan calls. *Do you object?*

Well, he makes the rest of us seem . . .

But he charms us. The syllables run

like vines in a baffling forest where

we've never been. His eyes look down

from the canopy. When he's called

to the blackboard, his letters have curious

tails, like fibery strands of meaning

coming loose. He sits at one side

toward the back, looks out at the starlings

bobbing and strutting on the grass.

What birds is he imagining? His eyes

settle on us, one by one, a tuft

of jungle feathers landing on a branch.

We come to class early, wanting to feel

the humidity change when Mario walks in.

Don't listen to Mario, the professor says.

But we do, his talk throatier, slurred,

faint drums and hungry insects underneath

the ornate Lisbon churches in the text,

the situation at the travel desk,

the doctor's office. Mario

is what we came for, we now believe.

We lose verbs and pronouns somewhere

in the underbrush. We may fail the course.

Students. Students. The language

has rules, conventions, idioms.

Mario does not resist. He studies, takes

the tests. But we can't seem to hold on

to the bank. We slip into some tributary

of the Amazon, slow swirls and eddies,

silt of a continent drifting toward

the sea, and in our ears Mario's dark

Portuguese, snakes tangled in tree roots,

bats dodging and dipping, now that it's

nightfall, out of the cave of his mouth.

MOON

Out of sight, on the step above

the curve in the stairs, the boy sits

listening to the fast, smart words.

Then the room quiets and they talk

about moon madness, sailors caught

in the full moon on a calm night,

how they might stare at the white

flesh pulsing on the waves

and step off into the sea. He crawls

up the stairs, a little dizzy, half asleep,

and there in his room the moonlight

slants through the window almost

to his bed. What would madness be?

He stands in the full moon, breathing,

his arms and belly whiter than he

has ever seen them. The moon, a yellow

eye with veins, looks only at him.
If he looks back . . . He looks.
He feels the yellow moving in,
seeping through his head and down

his spine. A one-eyed dog looks over
the roof of the house next door. He
can see its snout steaming and the cold
dripping from its mouth. The eye

says *come,* and he comes, drawn over
the snowy roofs, seeing it all
from above. He's not frightened,
it's some separate part of himself

moving away. The snow, with glimmers
from the houses, has become a sea,
rippling, reflecting yellow. A garage
tilts and begins to float. Then a touch

on his shoulder. A hand. His father
holding him. He's back in his room, small,
the moon still staring, eye
that will wait for him. And it does wait.

Years later that same moon, pale now,

hangs above the towers in New York City,

about to set at dawn. I wave for a cab,

give the address of the morgue.

Check in at the desk, I guess. Do they

wheel the body out or take me

into the chilled storeroom? I can't

remember. *Can you identify*—

they pull a sheet back from a face,

eyes and mouth open, cheek unshaved.

I nod, sign, and leave. Was that

my father's face, twisted, without

his glasses? Without his gentle poise.

It wasn't him—or me. The moon

reflects faintly in a bedroom

window. Then a cab draws up.

A BIRD

Two boys, a pile of sticks, a match—they send

a shaft of smoke, silver, twisting in

to the night, then watch the curved blade bend

above the trees and disappear. Gone.

Old friends die. Now a young one, a full-swing

dot-com mother, precise, lovely, heartsore,

finds that she's grown tired of everything

and dies. Our country hankers for a war.

Brancusi's *Bird in Space* is not a fowl

at all, but a cold knife, the shifty air

reduced to polished bronze. It doesn't fly,

it lasts. Once, its gleam could lift my eye

and hold it, breathless. Now its glare

mocks the night wind's broken howl.

NUMBERS

Waves in a November wind, elbowing

each other to be the next to go white,

curl, and fall. Yes, that appeals.

Or Houdini's mother, dead, hoping to find

a Ouija medium who knows enough

Yiddish to take a message to her Harry.

Satisfying. But how about the squares

and digits passing covert messages across

an equals sign? Numbers stand attentive

like Japanese children at a shrine,

but behind those neutral faces lie

reluctances and yearnings. Take *pi*.

Archimedes drew a polygon

inside a circle, measured, figured, found

the ratio: three and one seventh times,

rim to diameter. But *pi* shrugged off

that certainty. Its decimal places now

file off into the dark, a line of ants

waving antennae, signaling, as they shrink

to that hole where earth meets sky. Or take

ourselves, two small numbers multiplied

together. Coming to what? We're not sure,

not positive. Maybe we're *negative two.*

Then each of us may be a shadowy

square root, an elusive fugitive

camping out under a wind-blown tent.

Just as we suspected—take us one

by one, we turn imaginary, two thin

hypotheses, figures that students scribble

and erase, knowing we don't exist.

WINTER SOLSTICE

A child zips her boots, pulls on

her jacket and hat, and steps out

into the morning, dark as midnight.

Under the streetlight, she waits

for her friend. Waits. No one comes.

She walks through the new snow

toward school. Two cars pass, one

in each direction, tires squeezing

the ice. Light flickers in a house

and the news leaks out. As she passes

a tall hemlock, a furred blanket

of snow slides from a branch, a white

raccoon that may be following her.

A small wind has been angling

the snow down, but now it swirls

from behind the tree and calls up

a black dog almost as tall as she is.

They stop. Study each other.

The dog sniffs her arms, her belly,

looks up, trots on. She turns a corner

and there's a light over a door

and two boys walking toward it.

Her school. She's there. Holding

the dark around her, she finds

her room, her desk off by the black

window. A daytime voice comes

with its announcements, all for

someone else. As though

through glass, she watches

Ms. Paloma talking to the ceiling,

moving her hands. The teacher

doesn't see the girl and the dog,

the night, the heavy hemlock tipped

by the wind, the news spilling

on snow. For the girl, the dark

is like her father's car—she's in back.

They drive past the hands with pencils,

Ms. Paloma under a streetlight.

The class has studied it, the way

when the earth turns, a crack of light

comes under the eastern door. She

touches her father's neck. If he takes

a road to the west, fast as the earth

curls east, the dark will be hers.

VARIATIONS ON ANTONIO MACHADO'S "CAMINANTE"

Caminante, son tus huellas

el camino, y nada más;

caminante, no hay camino,

se hace camino al andar.

Al andar se hace camino,

y al volver la vista atrás

se ve la senda que nunca

se ha de volver a pisar.

Caminante, no hay camino,

sino estelas en la mar.

Traveler, your footprints

are the only path.

There is no road except

the one you make by walking.

Your steps create the road,

and looking back

you see the path

you'll never walk again.

For you there is no road

except a brief wake in the sea.

⊹

Catching a sheet of wind, the catamaran

tilts, lifts, loses the shore. With the taut

line in your fist, you lean back against a wave,

following twelve snow geese as they scrawl

a path across the sky. You're their sea shadow—

wake of air, wake of water, trailing and gone.

⊹

Cow knows her way

back to the barn. Feeling

her udder bulge, she humps up

from the river mud

and heads for her stall.

The mole digs with hands

in front of his head.

The long hole is home.

⊹

The Little Manistee is shallow

but fast, with a path of rocks

where kids jump their way

downstream. Two frogs hang

their chins on the surface.

Listen—the stichery song

of the yellowthroat. Memory

intact, those birds have flown

the old road, the air-trail

up from the Yucatan.

⁜

Thief, you want to lose those dogs?

Get your feet in the river. When your

smell's washed down over the rocks,

you'll be an innocent mist

somewhere upstream.

⁜

On the menu, you point to

Long Feng Pei.

The Chinese waitress checks

with the Chinese

chef. No one has ever ordered

Long Feng Pei.

Rinse your palette, lift vowels

to the roof

of your mouth, leave no footprints

in the *Long Feng Pei.*

⁜

You've wandered through parking lots and airports,

tunnels, fields of winter wheat and rape, wetlands,

shifting breasts of sand. Finally, your hand-woven

roads narrow to a cliff where every walker stands

to watch the midnight moon gather itself on the sea,

breaking, coming whole, shattering again.

⁕

Caminante, you can't go roadless.

You're following a woodchuck

to a tangled leg of swamp, but look

there where you're heading: footprints,

fireholes, broken shoes, a splash

of afterbirth in the weeds.

LET'S SAY
I'M SAD

Almost before I feel it, I find myself

saying it. *I'm sad.*

The feeling's like a shoe

tossed out of the rowboat,

it floats, then fills,

turns, drifts, sinks into the tangle

of weeds at the bottom. Right now, I'm

shoving that feeling

into words, watching it go down

as *sadness.* What would sadness be

without the word? I'll

step back, let my tongue go limp

and listen from the shore. There it is,

the feeling, still

as a carp in the muck. If it wants

to sulk there, breathing with its fins,

fine. Or if it craves,

maybe it will muscle up from the cold,

breach open-mouthed, and swallow

some wet wad of seeds.

Whatever. I'm just watching. Go,

sadness, find your own way.

When we first

walked upright, before we talked,

hunger must have been a huge

unopened need,

sadness vague and dark as the watery

shadow of a rock. No place for

carp. The word *carp,*

my hook to reel the blurred grief in.

OPEN

The open soul / is a lost soul . . .

—Dabney Stuart

Desultory air curls in, twists

on a pliant stem, moves on

to nudge the curtain and the late

begonias on the dresser. The soul

itself at season's end,

petals, phrases spoken somewhere—

or unspoken—touched by that circling

wind. Leaves folded back

like hands—giving or asking? Stem cut,

raked to the heap, some pollen flies

even now—even

in these autumn tailings.

Petals, no point in closing, around

what? The careless

equinox has taken it, song with a short

shelf-life, a child's hum or mine.

All lost in the fall:

scent, seed, the fine yellow dust

of spores, scattered down the unmarked

trails of the air.

Open. Hopeless and open.

    ⁜

Not like a book. Or the top of the red car

where a woman, waiting,

rests one hand on the wheel. Not an open

hearing, open house, open heart.

Open, instead, like Arizona

where the mountains shrugged,

turned north, and let the flat

land draw its own conclusions.

    ⁜

Soul hides in the colored

canyons of the brain—or valves,

veins, some hermitage

of flutes and fibers. Set free,

won't it ease out, breathe, drift

in eddies of the lean air?

It looks back, dreams back.

Through leaf-broken light

it almost recognizes gestures,

slants and sidesteps, handshakes,

my shrugs and stares. Too far—

can't make out the limp

and longing of companionable

flesh. But voice carries

even over distances like these,

half hoarse, hesitating,

doing my best to seem at ease.

Listening, does soul recall

long sadnesses, taut rope

raveling as we pulled

through a marsh of years—

and, over and under these,

the intricate entwinings,

meshing life with life?

The soul's not going back,

but still it clings, half hankering,

until an updraft scatters it.

A thread of road twists

by the river, and voices

blow downwind like smoke.

BLACK CAR BLUES

Like some black dog, that car smells out the street,

Nosing its way, that long car sniffs the street.

Why stop right here, long dog? You smell my feet?

I pour my sweet grease out the kitchen door,

My frying pan, I dump it out the door.

There goes my fat, I won't come back for more.

The cognac crowd, they hire a limousine,

The crowd prefers the long black limousine.

I flag the Amtrak, take the 9:15.

My woman loves her Tropicana juice,

Lots of pulp, my woman loves her juice.

Come on back here, we'll drink in the caboose.

One year was lucky—summer finally came,

A job, a neighborhood, a little fame.

The black car lurked and purred there, just the same.

You broil up a long black Cajun fish,

I like the way you fork that Cajun fish.

I don't much like another long black dish.

They've hung a stoplight on the avenue,

A brass stoplight at Rachet and Purdue.

Red or green, the black car rolls right through.

A man in black steps out around the car,

A man in black around the long black car.

He bows, he smiles, he asks us how we are.

I don't say much, my words roll up inside,

I let him smile, he claims he's on my side.

The night wind's quick. I'd rather walk than ride.

BLESSING
THE ANIMALS

At five today, the priest will bless

the animals, so we collect

on the stone rim of the fountain, old women

with canary cages, children holding

cats and parrots, a bowl of fish,

dogs, of course, some combed and ribboned,

others big and dour as burros. One boy

pulls a goat on a rope, another slides

a snake around his neck. We nod or talk,

cheerful, half serious about this rite

where no sins slouch in the shadows,

a baptism of the innocents.

                       By and by

the priest comes out,

a cream-colored robe with gold

embroidery. We gather, lifting

the animals, but he doesn't seem

to see us. He takes out a small book

and reads some words we can't

make out. Slips a carved stick

into a clay bottle, sprinkles

a little water on the nearest fur

or feathers, turns, and walks

back in. That's it.

                    All right,

Padre, maybe there is no scriptural

authority for blessing animals.

Maybe splashing water on a goat

is not your notion of a holy office.

Maybe you intend to teach

some dignity to your young

seminarian who thinks his calling is

to take the hands of wrinkled widows

on the street.

                    As we walk away,

a quick wind catches the fountain,

dissolves us all in mist. When it clears,

the finches and macaws fluff up their greens

and crimsons, tilt their heads, and add

their heathen whistles to the slippery skin

of water on the ancient stones.

AFTER-MUSIC

The mariachis now are skeletons.

Fancy hats still shade their skulls

and vacant mouths fall open,

singing. Here on a slab outside

the iron fence, I listen. The bone-lipped

trumpet shapes the old tune now,

then voices hollow out

the words—*allá donde vivía.*

These skeletons are young men, recklessly

off key. Up north our bones are dour,

pinned up for anatomy

or bagged in plastic for the coroner.

No sugar skulls or fiddles show us how

to rattle out the after-music.

Some of our dead still speak

but solo and sorry and seldom from

the pelvis. No high-pitched cry. No

rancherita. No bony digits quick

on the strings. No wired jaws

still longing after the tongue is gone.

TWO How the Juices Leap

OBOE

Your lips move moist around

my double reed, and I feel

the sad wind rising

through your throat. Some child

of yours is lost. If I were your

psychiatrist, I'd listen,

nod, prescribe. Instead,

I take your breath, shape it, let it find

a passage down this wooden

shaft, curl out around the ankles

of the clarinet. The horns

have forged a monumental

fountain on the stage and now

the strings supply the water,

surging up, looping, falling in

great sobs. The audience is weeping,

but you and I have doubts.

We wind our fiber through

the latticework of their grand art,

hoping someone may hear

the muscled twist

of grief that's seasoned

in a narrow tube, the hollow

music of a long-held breath.

EGG

You pass me from palm

to palm, run your eye along

my effortless asymmetry.

You handle me, knowing

my chalky curves

were turned on a lathe

of light. Palm to palm.

Before you make the next

move, do I remind you

of another yolk wrapped

in fragile bone, shapely,

golden in the center?

Do you recall how easily

a form you held

can crack and spill,

how absolute the absence?

POKER

Tongs open up into a laugh, remembering

they caught the live coal

in their jaws when Prometheus

first tossed it down. Somewhere they

roast an ox, heap up the fire.

And me? For a while I poked some logs.

Now I slouch here in the corner

watching the cabin give itself

to squirrels and roaches. The spider

I think of as my soul

climbs the cold chimney pipe,

finds it tarred at the roof, spins out

a line, and drops back down. That's

my spiritual adventure.

You might think the boys

in some back room would honor me

when they deal out their pairs

and flushes. I could suggest a ritual:

whenever a hand goes *straight,*

they might think of me, the unbent iron.

They might take off their hats.

No chance. I'm dust and ashes.

Rust. If I could find my heart

I'd pierce it, run it through.

CLUE

Toffee with tooth marks, the petal

of hibiscus that never blooms

this far north, a scrap of toenail,

those are my cousins. I'm the left-handed

slash here on your kitchen door,

the stroke that missed, before you

sank the knife and caught your breath

there at the sink, your blouse

splattered with good riddance.

Believe me, I'm not blowing

any whistles. We've been acquainted

only since last Friday, but I can

feel some new air edging in

around your bed, your kitchen table.

The cabin settles into sumac

and the dog sleeps. Another clue

might roll its eyes

or lean a little toward the camera.

Not me. I'm just a slash

in old paint. If homicide shows up,

I'll drape a spider web

across my loin. But I'll be here,

the child of rage, your child.

Touch my deep diagonal, leftover

lightning. Follow my falling line

into the larger dark.

Even the bitterest rain

can sink into sand, collect in

the crevasses of rock, and lose

itself in the river's

lurch and surge and pause.

PASSENGER-SIDE MIRROR

I glance over my shoulder,

a plainclothesman

letting you know what's lurking.

But you prefer to look

ahead, one hand on the wheel,

taking that curve below

the carved-out rock, moving in

whatever lane you choose.

You think a mirror's function

is to let you see the day receding,

everything you've crossed

or skirted diminishing behind you—

the flag girl there

in the construction zone, the slanted

Citroen easing toward its exit.

Objects in mirror . . . You ignore

my messages. Remember

that school bus you passed? It's

not far behind us, five children's faces

in the windshield. And the smoking

pickup? It never did turn off.

While you've been terracing

the hills and parceling out

the bottomland, I've watched it

coming on, this huge blue fender,

inches from my face.

CHERRY PIE

We're all acquainted with the airy

crowd—a stalk of celery dipped

in cottage cheese, a thimble

of soy milk, a few green grapes.

I invite them over here: between

two butter crusts, my sour

flesh so deeply sugared it

astounds the mouth.

To coax it all to bed, a downy

pillow of whipped cream.

Try me, you organics.

Light the oven.

Let me show you how

the juices leap, when nature

shares the sheets with art.

QUATRAIN

There's villanelle walking around,

retreating, a small bell echoing on

each ankle. Perched on the power line

are seven haikus, introspective, wan,

each one remembering a certain

cherry tree or golden carp

or thread of water down a rock.

And there's sestina in the park

shelling peanuts for her six

tame squirrels—each one takes a nut

and stays for her next stanza. Tall

in the evening light stands sonnet

under the courthouse pillars, fourteen

steps above the street. Me,

I never settled down. I rattle

on through town, waving to Bonnie

Barbara Allan, my old acquaintance,

still alive, pacing the graveyard.

My track curves below the free-verse

runnels, each one trying hard

to be a river. My wheels clack

over the ties, the rusting rails.

I take it slow, knowing I'm crammed

with crates of paint and pistols, bales

of fodder, motors that breathe oxygen

and oil. I am a box hitched

to a box hitched to a box, snaking

across the territory, switched

off the main line, bridging, tunneling,

turning up. I see the dock

and depot waiting to take me in.

They forget: I'm rolling stock.

MOUSTACHE

Hair up on top is white, but I'm

as dark as thirty—

a relic, a reminder. Eyes,

cheeks, and the other hangers-on

are in decline. Only

words have kept their resonance.

So, words, remember I'm

the formal awning under which

you signal for a cab,

the well-trimmed doorman, bowing

slightly, ushering you out.

If things go well, I'll look on

as your slippery diphthongs

warm the room, as you tuck

a metaphor in among the shrimp

and grape leaves. I like

the way you stroke me with your

consonants, but before

the evening's gone, you'll slip

back to stories

from another neighborhood

where once, in church,

you threw yourself away

and spoke in tongues. I wish

I'd known you then, your open

vowels and silences,

the ledge of your bare lips.

ALARM CLOCK

I'm here, indoor cricket

clicking you to sleep. Our pulses,

sixty even, straighten out the night.

I wake you—four quick beeps—

though I'd rather watch you

roll and mutter through some urgent

dream. Your thank-you

is to blip me on the head, male

hormones coming on at dawn

out of some ancient cave.

Evolution has its say, I guess.

I forgive you that. I know we're

different species, but I can't resist.

I keep offering my open face,

my nightly whisper

by your unshaved cheek.

No luck. That woman slips

under your sheet, and I

ache here on the windowsill.

I know I should hunt out

a mate of my own kind—

your shaver, maybe.

I can't do it. I'm cursed

with an unnatural affection.

RUNOFF

Hopeless weekends dripping

from the sky, notarized

lies, winged seeds, the arm

and eyelid of a doll—all this

is me, sloshing, taking my time—

bones of the banker rolled

in a green wind. Pablo Neruda,

my uncle, pours his sexual

water in my cracked cup. *Ruido*

rojo de huesos. Beetles roll

to the inhale of my blood—

whatever seeps from the lungs

of leaning houses, what percolates,

what shouts, what hugs the broken

post of its love. In a bad time,

when you're choking on smart

bombs and stupid ones,

I'm here to reassure you.

Aceite sin nombre. Your steel

towers, horn concertos,

blizzards, hairdos, sirens,

poems, palms, CDs, DVDs

SUVs—that's my lineage,

sloping down. Rain falls,

cracked clouds spill their

guttered news,

I take it all in my arms.

HUNCH

Never mind the safe municipal

that claims to offer 3.8%

for fifteen years. Forget

the charts that promise you

the intracoastal channel

when the tide goes out. No

memorizing everything the deck

has dealt. Just follow me

into the tall grass swale

here by the woods. See the way

the sun gets broken

in that patch of swamp?

The way that droop of juniper

makes a doorway

to the dark? Soon you'll hear

the insects' smooth roulette

clicking out your name.

Inside this mound

I carry on my back, some ancient

bones are buried, a trove

where low life stirs,

where larval broods ferment

and generate. Put your hand here

where my humped shoulders

bend to the ground. Feel

the current? That's the fingernail

of luck, crawling up your arm.

NEGATIVE SPACE

Where the body isn't—that's how

dancers know me. Sculptors bend

their clay and steel against

my emptiness. Somehow, though I'm

not giving it a thought, I nudge

a shadow from a twist

of bronze or change the way

a breast and elbow size

each other up. Writers like to wrap

white space around their wit,

but I'm not white,

not bound or folded. I'm your

zero with its circumference

erased, an abandoned building

once the building's gone. Let's say

a heavy childhood event

has bent your life, shaped

what you've become. Now you find

it never happened. Nothing

there at all. That's me.

MOUSETRAP

My parents were mousetraps

and my grandparents, an ancestry

of wood and wire. I knew my trade.

You should have seen me half

a century ago. Cocky. *Build a better*

mousetrap, someone would say.

I'd look him in the eye. *Some things*

are what they are, I'd say.

Can you build a better guillotine?

The blade falls—gravity with an edge.

Want to try a circular saw?

That was the way I talked back then.

Now I waste here on the shelf

behind the d-CON. No offspring,

end of the line. Still, after midnight,

I can feel my wire go taut

against the headboard, my curled

hips ready. I wait,

pretend to sleep. When something chews

the cheese between my legs,

everything I've stored

breaks free. The job is done,

done right. I draw a breath, lean back,

sleep out the night.

ELECTRIC
COLLAR

I'm the cop you've hired

to enforce your petty ordinance.

Whenever Jessie races

toward the street beyond

the planted wire, I have to shoot

these bolts of fire

to her throat. But I love

that six-month hound. All day, I rub

the soft hairs of her neck

and she murmurs news

of everything under the leaves

and on the wind. These shocks—

as if someone made you whip

your daughter for roller-skating

in the park. I have a plan.

Tonight I'll burnish up my brass,

unwrap my arms from Jessie's neck,

and snake my way into your

jewelry box. While you're considering

an item to set off your blouse,

I'll curl my languid leather

underneath your hand.

You'll take me to your throat

a Gucci touch, discreetly

punk. Then we'll step out—

high fashion, night air cool and moist,

and the streetlight, waiting.

SMALL GRAY BOX WITH THREE WIRES

We've all seen bodies when

the brain is gone. I'm the opposite,

intelligence unplugged,

waiting on the basement shelf.

Something's staggering without me,

but I can't remember what.

I swapped the circuits, forked

the frequencies, didn't notice

what the arms and wheels

might be doing. Some machine

must miss me. But here, deserted, I

become the latest species—

a free-ranging brain. I'll find out

what conspiracies may be

fermenting in your

cellar, what's folded in your

ferny fractals. I'm the celestial

weasel sniffing out

black holes. Hello, whose are

those blurred pikes

and pixels? A collusion!

Messy but I pull them up,

stash the squinting evidence.

You need some proof?

Here, Spade, I'll show you

where to dig, once I get my

glockles on the grid.

DEAF EAR

I watch a motorcycle smoking

on the street, tree tops wrestling,

some soprano hollowing

her arms and breasts and lips

around a body on the stage—

and, with them, no sound,

whatever that may be.

Mostly, I'm content. Seeing

is enough. But now I'm walking

a Nebraska road, at dawn,

before the cars have found it.

Over there, a square white house,

two pines, a shed and silo.

Four cows sleep in an endless

field. A full moon settles

west beyond a stand of timber,

and along a disappearing

line of fence, a dogwood

eases into bloom.

I see and breathe. No single

smell drifts in, but still

I take the scent of prairie

absences. Now I believe:

another door could open

on this emptiness. I long for it,

your huge countryside of silence.

WANING MOON

I rise at midnight when the first

sleep staggers into dream.

Later and lesser. In a week

I become the dark.

My music knows its way

to a Nash rusting by a shed,

the slow mating of snakes

in the creek bed. My half-moon

blues, my strum on the two

lanes of an empty road—

the road you're following

beside some dusty milkweed

and the fence. I draw my bow

across the telephone wires,

a thin dirge

for your nation, for the end

of something wild,

broad backed, generous.

Listen for me. With help

from the wind, I can pour

my six pale notes

through the night's sieve,

lend you the crickets' cadence

to walk home by.

THREE   Steering by Pheromones

EARLY STORM

Pared down, defoliated, bare

(the way they should have been), the trees

would have shrugged off this sudden freeze—

October lightning, sleet, the flare

of power lines, and the wet sky

miscarrying these globs of snow.

They've stuck a finger in the eye

of storms before. But up there, now,

ten thousand leaves are dawdling in

a vague midsummer haze, green, full,

their hands held out for one more nickel

from their reckless Uncle Rain.

Night and ice—limbs crash down,

trunks split, the lights blow out.

Grown old, we're still not used to it:

slow ripening, then cold-too-soon.

A CLUTCH
OF MAMMALS

I check the dark canal for manatees

and find them sometimes, great

sea cows, hot tubbers lolling here,

hides murky except for white propeller scars

or a patch that might be lichen

there behind the eye. They draw me,

five bodies rolling in a lethargy

of longing, drifting down

to chew the bronzy weeds, I guess,

then lifting their nostrils, three pairs in a row,

to sneeze out stale air

and suck some sultry oxygen

back in. They fluke the surface, while I perch

on the concrete ledge,

hoping to slide my bare foot down

some belly flesh. Which part of me,

which self, drifts over

every evening, ready to slide in

among the mermaids? They allure me,

draw me under.

In the salty dark, we're moved by some

shapeless desire—no barracuda lust

for flesh, no migratory

edict driving us to thrash

and leap upstream. The open sea blows huge

out there, white circles

curling on the crest of waves

like eyes that notice momentarily

our piece of shore—a rocking

catboat, mangroves, an egret hunkered

on a post. The eyes dismiss us and are gone.

Left behind, we wheel

in the shallows, hide to hide.

No fancy principles. Hot water bubbling

from a power plant?

We'll take it. Or a sad canal

like this one, a place to duck away from blades

and the metal roar that twists

the glancing symmetries we knew.

We're a clutch of mammals, not that cold codfish

dropping five million eggs

in mid-Atlantic, hoping some traveling

sperm will find them out. A vegetable

lassitude leads us

to drifting strands of chlorophyll,

an underwater meadow where we graze,

weightless ruminants,

upended, chewing the ends of time.

PATH TO
THE CABIN

I know the way to the cabin. But this moonless

night the dark's so thick you breathe it, brush

against its dense black fur. The path curves,

but which way? I stumble into a hemlock limb,

some thorny bush. The other way then. Roots.

The muttering of a stream I had forgotten.

A couple of rocks to cross on, but where

are they? Where is the stream itself? Cicadas

shout from the trees. Frogs chunk. The creek's here

somewhere. Looking up, I see a thin

strip of sky between the trees. If I

could follow that ragged map—looking

straight up while I walk—would I find

the path? I fall on a stump and catch myself

wrist deep in its rotted center. At the lodge,

fifteen minutes ago, I played Ping-Pong,

making a few good shots, scooping the ball

almost off the floor or leaning in

and slamming it to the far left corner. I lost

to the supple woman who kept returning

everything, but some of the old technique

came back. Here I shuffle, hands out, blind

except for the fireflies, each waving a quick

goodbye as I turn to look. Katydids

call now, inviting someone, and still

the undertow of crickets—a night of creatures

steering by pheromones through the sexual

dark. Down here on all fours,

I'm asking for a whiff of where to go.

SCRAMBLE COMPETITION POLYGYNY

In the spring, female horseshoe crabs

wait in the bay until

the tide and moon are right, then come ashore—

all of them at once—to spawn.

The males hang around

low water, loitering. When a female shoots

the rocky shallows, headed for

the beach, the quickest male

grabs on and rides her up the sand—no slow dance

in the undertow, no caudal spine

curling and saluting,

just sperm hopping on the egg train.

Wood frogs, too, become receptive

just one night of the year.

When males smell that dark approaching,

they slouch around the pond—dozens,

hundreds of them—

muttering in the mud, ready. Out

of the woods, on low hops, come the females

and the orgy's on.

Let them be crabs and frogs, without thinking

Fort Lauderdale or prom night.

That's what distinguishes

a biologist—it's just *scramble competition*

polygyny, nothing to get

nervous about, no glimpses

of daughters beached or grandsons slimy

with pond mud. No memories of yourself

as warty frog in shallow

water, splashed and blinking,

jumping on the heap, finally—

voice garbled and gone.

DUST MITES

No need to wait to be reborn in your next life. You are

being reborn as you read, reincarnated only to crawl

away on thousands of tiny legs.

—ROBERT DUNN, "Wild Beneath the Sheets:

A Bestiary of the Miniscule," *BBC Wildlife Magazine,*

September 2003

Our scraps of talk, the nips,

pleas, undercuttings, the threats

and sighs have shrunk now

out of sight, millions of mites, invisible.

Yet as the dust drifts and settles, they find

our cast-off skin, tiny jaws still chewing.

⁂

A boy hides in the dark closet,

the voices fading finally. He stands

in someone else's clothes, woolen,

smelling of sweat. He feels

the dust mites sealing his eyes and ears.

⊹

"House dust is not dust after all. It is, it turns out,

mostly mites and human skin. House dust is

alive."

⊹

My pillow shifts and stirs—feathers

nudging themselves into a V

and flying south, so I had supposed.

Now I know better. A tenth

of this pillow's heft is mites

alive and dead. A small churning,

but they find the climate here

conducive. They intend to stay.

⊹

We're off to Spinalonga and down

the coast to Aghios Nikolaos—

lobster boats, motor bikes, bare flesh

on the beach, air rattling with words

we'll never understand. Then east

to Itanos, where the island's tail

slaps the sea. At the world's end,

we lie down on a narrow bed

and feel the old life underneath us,

a miniscule metropolis,

eating, mating, laying eggs.

⊹

"Forget Yellowstone, the call of the wild is in your

bed, though not in the way you thought."

⊹

Finding each other on the rug,

touching, rising, coming

together in a burst of breath,

we feel a certain pride

as though our loving deserves

an audience. We have one.

Ten thousand mites clack

their pinchers, wave their tiny tail hairs.

⊹

The dryer groans downstairs, squirrels

run on the metal roof, someone's getting

dramatic on the phone. With all this racket,

how can I hear the munch and murmur

of the dust, curling where the sun slants in?

THE FLY

Embedded in redundancies,

we find it hard to believe:

one source of information, one

response. A fly, sucking the juice

of roadkill, feeds until its crop

is swollen, bulging. Then

a single nerve flags down

the brain: *Enough already. Stop.*

And what if that nerve is severed?

We want to tell the fly, Wait.

Use a few facets of your compound

eye. Look back at that enormous

bladder, dragging there behind you.

What do you think that weight is,

bending your hind legs down?

But, no, the fly keeps on feeding

and the crop explodes. We feel

superior. We would have noticed

even if one nerve were cut.

But then we think of instances.

Our species, too. We put our head

down in the roadkill, taste the juice,

feed and feed until our crop explodes.

HIPPOCAMPUS

In a day, a chickadee can cruise the neighborhood

and hide three hundred seeds in crevasses

in bark or moss, never a spot he's used

before. Weeks later, hungry, he looks, remembers,

finds the seeds, and eats. Better yet,

Clark's nutcracker, in the fall, can dig

nine thousand holes in a hillside, hide pine seeds

in each and cover up each cache. His memory,

housed in the hippocampus, will hold

eight thousand of those indistinguishable

spots and feed him through the winter

and the spring. What about another species,

us? Not so good at stashing and recalling,

but on a city street we pass

a thousand faces, all looking straight ahead

behind their scarves, and in a dreaded instant

recognize the one we hoped had gone
to Istanbul—or, glimpsed obliquely
through the snow, a twist of hair and forehead
that we almost married. Even in a reckless

photograph of sixteen sepia girls
a century ago we can pick out
the face we came for. Our hippocampus must
be weighted down with slopes and shadings,

eyebrows, noses, cheeks, half-parted lips, a bit
of ear—configurations of our fears
and loyalties and longings, seeds we hide away
and feed on, week by week, all winter long.

EXITS

Endangered creatures—let's say

the House of Lords or the Ku Klux Klan—

may find their habitat has shrunk

and they're about to disappear.

They know they're going, and they won't

go quietly. Others, like blacksmiths,

barbers, boatwrights, shoeshine boys

just turn up missing. We hardly notice

when their patch of woods is condoed

into Woodland Grove. Now you

and I put on our gaudy plumage

and whistle the odd and varied call

we've always used to claim a territory

and a mate, choosing not to notice

that our luscious bit of swamp—

cattails, water striders, schooling

fry—has just become the rough

on the seventh hole. I saw something

in a book not long ago: three cranes

in a snowy landscape, small cranes,

shapely, delicate, with a red spot

somewhere about their heads—

a few dozen left, if I remember right.

Their rarity somehow refined

the calligraphic rise of their necks.

They stood aloof, unwilling to raise

a clamor for their lost cause. Where is

that book? I'd like to check their names,

the snow, that spot of red.

FOUR One Match Flaring

WISE MAN

No one here is old enough. The father,

if that's what he is, stands awkward as a stork.

The mother does not know whether to smile

or cry, her face beautiful but ill-defined

as faces of the young are. Even the ass

is a yearling, and the sheep mutter like children.

To whom shall I hand this myrrh that has trailed

its bitter breath over the desert?

I am tired of mothers and their milky ways,

of babies sticky as figs. I have left a kingdom

of them. There must be some truth beyond

this sucking and growing and wasting away.

A star should lead an old man, you would think,

to some geometry, some right triangle

whose legs never slip or warp or aspire

to become the hypotenuse. Instead, this star

wandering out of the ecliptic has led us

to dry straw, a stable, oil burning in

a lamp, a mother nursing another mouth.

Creation, then, is the only axiom—

and it declines to spell itself across

the sky in Roman letters. Some events

are worth a journey, but there are no

abstract fires or vague births. Each fire

gnaws its own sticks. The welter of what is

conspires in this, a creation you can hold

in your hands, a child. A definite baby

squalls into life, skids out between the legs

of a definite woman, bedded in straw, on the longest

night of the year. And a certain star burns.

JOSEPH

Yes, sure, the Holy Ghost.

That happened to my cousin too.

A windy day—got caught in a cloud

of celestial pollen.

It happens from time to time,

especially to the pure ones.

White flowers seem to invite

the holy bees. But then this dream.

I dream all the time. Some man stops me,

says I owe him a white goat,

or dogs howl behind the house

and the whole village comes to listen.

But this dream was clear

and short: no stoning, no divorce.

A son. Well, all right. Who knows

how the fine dust drifted.

Maybe he'll be good at cutting

and planing. I can use some help. Besides,

Mary—well, you've seen her.

I know when I've been lucky. Now

it's Caesar Augustus, taxes, Bethlehem.

We'll make it, Mary

on the mule—Mary and son—

and me walking. Mary beautiful, as the full

moon rises. Mary,

my wife, and the dream,

that clear one, with the angel talking. . . .

THE ANIMALS

If sheep are sheep, if holiness does not
apply to them, why do they crowd around
the straw where Jesus lies? Why do we draw
them in? We need the oily smell of fleece,
the ox stamping and breathing, the ass
rubbing his rump against the stall.

Taxes, a journey, strange men on camels,
a star—this is too thin a tale to carry half
of history on its back. It needs the urgency
of birth and something hooved and hairy
that won't be gone when the Word
is slurred in some fanatic wind.

We need muscle yoked to the furrowing
earth and a dry stretched hide where we
can beat the rhythm of our love.

ADAM'S CHRISTMAS

Too small to know a gift

or give one. Too new

to understand

annunciation, a peculiar

star, a crowded inn.

Like the first Adam,

you're setting out to name

the colors, faces, lights—

this blurred and lushly

peopled garden—

before any of it

needs to be redeemed.

THE WOMAN
FROM CHIAPAS

Except for the eyes, who would know her?

Eyes narrow and still and hard in a broad

face, eyes young enough to be resigned

and furious at the same time. The mother

from Chiapas—we guess she's seventeen—

holds her child in a blue rebozo, his

nose flat against her blouse, his face

dark. The child, when he is grown,

may become a storyteller, a man

that men and women follow—grave,

graceful, and forgiving. But the woman

has seen grace terrify the bosses

and make them brutal. She looks at us

steadily. She foresees and does not forgive.

CHRISTMAS, MEXICO

December here, with sun and the faint smell

of wood smoke in the air—

a late September day. The jasmine drops

a few last blooms; limes swell

and ripen, one by one, outside the door.

Dusk comes a little earlier.

Here, we will have months or years to eat

the apple of our hearts down

to the dark seeds. How leisurely the fall.

How slow the holy cold comes on.

SCRIPT
FOR A COLD
CHRISTMAS

These reds and greens, of course, are all wrong—

the blazing log, the star like a sunflower

almost toppling the tree. All fall, the colors

have been diminishing. Look: the beech tree

breathes twigs of vapor against the gray sky,

icicles drop their spindly light in a long beard

from eaves to bush to ground. My promises

have cracked and dropped away like old bark.

I am a winter stick, a flagpole clanging

a hollow note in the wind. There is nothing

dramatic here, neither jubilation

nor despair, but rather a kind of exile

as when in a foreign country you shrink

into yourself, unable to speak.

Our rituals exaggerate. The star

was no Catherine wheel spinning and hissing

over the stable. It was a star, a point

of no dimension, one match flaring across

a frozen lake. The shepherds, hearing the angels'

song, thought it was the wheeze of a cold sheep

it had so thin a sound. They heard but hardly

spoke, saving their words like a last handful

of grain. And the child—one child, not a crèche

in every park. This one was different,

but not yet. Now it was a small jug

of flesh with a candle glimmering inside.

It is almost cold enough. The year is shrinking

toward a small festival, a saturnalia

that will fit in the cavity of a tooth.

We may gather up our deaths and make

of them a twig fire, hold our hands

to it, and sing for the cold seed.

ELEVATOR MUSIC

Above the strings, the tenor pauses,

catches his breath, slurs and sighs

in his dreamless sleep, while we pass

kitchenware, bed and bath, then rise

to lingerie and Xmas seasonals.

Meanwhile, in Palestine, the razor-

wire cuts, families crumble,

another death cries out for

suicide. What ceremony

is this, then? What do we celebrate

with fleece and flickering light? The day

grows burdensome and dark and late,

the door slides shut. I want to ride

this shaft back down, past *lower level,*

to the place where rocks grind out their low

tectonic music, notes that might tell

what happened on that longest night—

an agonizing birth, thin

starlight, mother, child—and gifts

from some far country, freely given.

CHRISTMAS NIGHT

Let midnight gather up the wind

and the cry of tires on bitter snow.

Let midnight call the cold dogs home,

sleet in their fur—last one can blow

the streetlights out. If children sleep

after the day's unfoldings, the wheel

of gifts and griefs, may their breathing

ease the strange hollowness we feel.

Let midnight draw whoever's left

to the grate where a burnt-out log unrolls

low mutterings of smoke until

a small fire wakes in its crib of coals.

MIDNIGHT

That boy won't go to sleep—dancing,

clowning, chewing the edges

of night—until his mother straps

him in the car and drives. Glancing

patterns: storefronts, Christmas deer

outlined in lights. He leans back

and seems to concentrate, breathing

in the dark where faces disappear,

nothing to be hankered for

or lost, no place to go, only

gears clutching—second, third, fourth—

easing him forward then back once more,

acceleration all mixed up

with gravity. Eyes roll, head tilts,

and he's asleep, rocked in the cradle

of the motor age, and on the tape

Art Tatum's liquid touch, not loud,

syncopated with the wingless flight

of streetlights headed south—what sleep

has always been, snow-boughed

shapes outside a window, a swirl

that by morning may be plowed and heaped

but now is shifty, drifting and blown.

The sleeper's fingers stretch and curl

as he might reach in a shadowed stream,

feeling for weeds, then going under

to touch the red fins of the fish

that swim the midnight flux of dream.

DECEMBER 26

At dawn, sun-glints ricochet from drift

to drift, tree shadows reach and tangle

on the sloping snow. Wind lifts

a fine spray, a silken scarf that glistens,

frays, and is gone. Cornerless,

the neighborhood forgets its long

division, the angles, edges, overhangs

that used to curb our streets.

The blue-crab world has cracked

its shell wide open, and we touch

new skin, like a pear's flesh, white

and sinewy. The crab backs out,

working its pale fingers loose from

the old pincers, stares at the brittle

boat abandoned on the sand, and knows

it may be eaten. Still it takes the sunlight

on its nakedness, stretches,

shuttles sidewise into what's to come.

SHEPHERD

There was music in that barren place

already. While sheep grazed, the thin clank

of bells hung about them like a mist. Above,

we listened to that hollow clatter—no beat,

no tune, but a tinny music sweet as crickets.

And of course we knew the stars. At night

we'd find a rock that had stored up some warmth,

lean back, and name the sky as it crept west.

But the star that night—a fleck of white fire

low in the east, an open eye. And music

like voices calling, sinking in crevasses

behind us, and calling again. No wind

could make that sound, and there was no wind.

We set out in a sort of trance. And found . . .

what? An ordinary child, I guess—

a lamb bleary with birth. But music still hung

on the air like the sharp smell of sage

at the first of spring. We stood silent awhile,

then climbed back to our rocky ledge,

lay in the cold and watched the ancient shapes

circling: the serpent and the scorpion,

the bear sniffing around the pole, the fish,

the greater and the lesser dog, the ram—

and the milky road across the dark.

FIVE   Bird with the Downcast Beak

SELF-PORTRAIT
AS WATERFALL

I've been following

this creek bed all my life—

boulders, cattails,

water striders—a thin

meander. When you appear

on the path below,

the cliff gives

into empty air and I fall,

glancing off the limestone,

catching scraps

of sunlight through the sycamores.

Did you know you held

gravity in your hand?

My slow drift

shatters to this broken

light swung sidewise

by the wind. Gathering

myself in a weedy pool,

I offer you two frogs,

three lilies opening into bloom,

and over on that log

a hunched green heron.

FINDING
THE WAY

Plenty of palmy avenues

labeled Peninsula or Lakeside

Circle, but no sign of the lake—

unless that patch of water through

the redwood fence . . . ? And wasn't it

the *ocean* we were looking for?

Spanish tiled roofs, Spanish

moss dripping from what they call

oak trees, bromeliads in fancy

planters, hard little grapefruit dropped

in the grass. A gardener shinnies up

a palm and chops dry fronds

so they won't clutter up the pool.

No landmarks. Just miles of tidy self-

congratulation. At the end

of some no-outlet boulevard,

there must be water, but I've even

lost the Tamiami Trail.

They've moved the tuna fish. And why

isn't olive oil here with the canola?

The vegetable man says he hides

the Fordhook lima beans in that freezer

just beyond the pillar—so that, for customers

who really want them, they'll be there.

That's me. Maze of alleys,

desert of pop and pretzels, artificial

dog bones. Looking for black-olive

hummus, I stray off into Top Job,

Vanish, and The Works. Maybe some

thighs or gizzards and then I'll find

my check-out girl, the one who's fast

and sullen. We speak only of

the winter day or the missing price tag

from the tangerines, but handing

the pen over and back, we sign

a kind of pact. When the first blizzard blows,

we'll ask each other's name, pull jackets up,

and duck into those aisles of twisting snow.

※

In our rented jeep, we leave the hard road

south of Kambi, slope down past

a whitewashed chapel with its arch

and bell, past two windmills like old

salt cellars with splintered roofs

and huge wheels, just wooden spokes now

wingless and unturning. Then boulders,

pines—we take it slow, wondering if this

is road or riverbed. Over a rise:

the sea, deeply Aegean. We angle

down, drawn over shifty rocks

by that magnetic blue. The beach

is almost empty, we are late

and lost. A solitary sunbather

looks up, comes over to the jeep,

bare breasted, leans her tan hands

on the door, looks us over, points

to a rutted trail that might take us back.

If going back was what we wanted.

CRETE: THE DIKTAEAN CAVE

Swallows careen into the cave and out,

children daring each other

at dusk. Behind us the opening glows

with a green light, like a smell from the past—

then the dark, except for candles

and their faltering shadows. We see

the ledge where the baby Zeus was stowed,

hidden from his father,

Kronos, who thought he had eaten him.

We blow the candles out and stand, silent,

in the stone room,

the walls moving in, the air dead.

Absolute dark. They say that bees flew here

to bring Zeus

honey, that she-goats came

to offer him their teats. Somehow the Greeks

knew, even then,

that under this mountain of rock,

a river of cold water flows, and farther

down, where stories

begin, the final room is fire.

DAUGHTER IN NEW YORK

You wanted art—and got it, five days

of the Fricke, the Guggenheim,

New Guinea's woven bowls and wooden

faces, Toulouse Lautrec, the Chelsea

galleries and what's left of Soho,

so many strokes and slashes, green-

shadowed bones and broken clumps of sky.

And evenings, after the art,

my brother called up glimpses

of our family, things I never knew

or never thought to mention.

Now you've heard my father's true-pitch

tenor and my brother's baritone,

me wobbling in between, you've

watched my mother measure out

the salt and Crisco to cook up

two sons by the book. I must have scenes

stored somewhere too. Our mother

in the sink-light listening

to Gabriel Heater mourn the war—

there's bad news tonight—

and outside the kitchen window

goldfish coming to life again

as the pool-ice thaws. A scene,

but what shape were her glasses, what

scarf or sadness was she wearing?

Upstairs a gooseneck lamp throws a tent

around the Underwood, its chrome-

rimmed keys sitting like students

in four strict tiers, waiting for what

my father had to say. But what

was it? I never sat in on his classes,

not even one. That was Ferndale.

We played touch football in the street,

came in to pot roast steaming in its grease,

a jacket tossed across a chair.

Jane, I needed you back then to brush

a blue reflection on a neck and arm,

to slant the table where mother

whipped potatoes, cradling the bowl

against her belly like a child.

BLOOD WORK

Elastic band above the elbow, a vein,

the needle, and three vials sucking it up,

dark red, almost black. The Small Bang

back there at the beginning, then this flux,

yeasty and mysterious. They've named

the liver, prostate, pericardium—

but still the anti-matter shifts its weight

from lobe to lobe. Proteins, enzymes,

the bad seed. The whole shebang is right here,

wrapped up in a yard or two of skin, and yet

the quarks and hadrons orbit on their own.

Strange to be so baffled by this soft

contraption I sometimes think of as my own.

I take the rowboat out on this small lake,

familiar coves and cottages, swamp grass,

a stream—the surface handing back the mottled

afternoon. I drop a hook and worm and sinker

knowing something's down there. Then night falls.

A scrap of moon is broken on the waves.

Off to the right, a loon throws its clear and throaty

mock across the water. It dives. Where to?

What weedy avenues must open if you

can read the dark. From far across the lake

the loon-voice, disembodied, calls again.

RADIATION

The seeds they plant around the gangling bush

are called *palladium*, a cheerful word,

alive with lights as though I'd feel a rush

of Cuban dancers in the groin, a bird

tossing a blue-green tail and whistling from

a dark Bolivian wood. Seeded, I might

expect a splash or two of bloom, the hum

of bees and beetles practicing some sleight

of wing to fertilize the lowlands. No,

my anti-seeds are promising a crop

of dust. A vegetable flame will grow

like kudzu from those radiant kernels, wrap

the local foliage in fire, trash

it, letting fall, I hope, some fertile ash.

THE VISIT

April afternoon. The concert master

comes to see his friend

one last time, rests the violin

against his neck, and lets Vaughan

Williams' lark climb

the feathered strings, slant off,

catch a lift from the west wind,

stroke into a long

diminuendo as ripe air

rises from a dogwood down below.

A dark sky

blows in as predicted, the bird

disappears, but the note still unfolds

like a strand of

blue-eyed grass nudged by rain.

HURTLE

It is possible to feel my life, in a quiet ecstatic helpless-

ness, as a long slow hurtle through the forms of things.

—Robert Hass

Eight years I ran the hurdles, with enviable

form but not much speed, those white rectangles

three steps apart. On the starting block

I looked down through the shrinking windows

to the end. The gun. The burst of muscle,

right leg out over the hurdle and the left

coming behind, reaching for the next white wood,

March-April-May parceled out in sixteen-second

afternoons. Since then, I hurtle slowly

through the forms of things, bewildered, now

and then ecstatic, a doorway in, a window

out. A garden promised on a full

white skirt, the far thin notes of a white-

throated sparrow. Can supper be a form?

Or a priest splashing dogs, canaries,

snakes with holy water? The formal rails

of a Spanish train, child broken, heart

trapped in dust. And then the wild and woven

birds of Otavalo. Now, I'm framed

by the cones of city lights that come on

one by one, reflecting from the glass

of empty shops. No traffic, but a yellow

blinker. I imagine I can see a thin

white ribbon where the street curves left.

NO CLOCKS

"How long do I have?" Dr. Blix doesn't hesitate,

surgeon of the prostate, who's seen

my numbers rise. "Five years."

※

As the day approached, John Donne

had his portrait painted in his winding sheet,

the heavy fabric tight around

his cheeks and beard, his eyes closed,

a knot of cloth on the top of his head.

※

I know death-too-soon,

the terrible empty room,

the broken stairs. My death

is the ordinary kind. Still, for me,

it will be an event.

※

Five fingers, one with a ring,

five curls of smoke

from a maple log,

five clear notes from

an oboe or a cello,

five words

under a gooseneck lamp.

⁕

From up on the Golden Gate Bridge,

I can see a ferry inching across the thin

white strings of waves that creep

toward shore. Falling from here,

a person would shrink, second

by second, until he became

a penciled comma on the sea.

⁕

When I gather you in,

loves of my life,

let's kneel around the fire

whose quick syllables

speak for the chimney wind.

The logs are wild black cherry,

limbs that fell in our yard.

⁕

In the eight-minute task, the flyer

winches his sailplane straight up

six hundred feet in the air. It weaves

upwind to find a thermal, lifts, slides

sideways, rides the good air almost

out of sight. With his eye on the clock,

he calls it down, circles it to burn off

the last scraps of time, brings it home,

drops it right here in the painted

circle, nose down, motionless, exactly

when his seconds are used up.

☩

I'll do a poem or puzzle

to keep my brain

upright so it can crouch

behind the body

as it swerves and rackets

down the slope.

☩

Since I am coming to that holy room

  Where, with Thy choir of saints forevermore,

I shall be made Thy Music, as I come

  I tune the instrument here at the door,

  And what I must do then, think now before.

Well, Donne, maybe so. I'll trim a reed,

breathe a B-flat down this hollow tube,

just in case.

☩

Blix, what regimen do you suggest? You're factual

and certain, proud to be forthright.

You're young

but not so young as Emelie, my slender

student, back from Senegal.

She writes,

"There will be no clocks. Death itself

is enough, the impossible

certainty of it,

clinging to us like wet dirt."

PELICAN

I sought his Lodging, which is at the Signe

Of the sad Pelican.

> —ANDREW MARVELL, "Fleckno, an English
>
> Priest at Rome"

The city thinks it knows you by your sign,

bird with the downcast beak, sad pelican,

but you can wing it, glide above the brine,

letting your hunger ride a ten-foot span.

Here on the street, you listen to the whine

of carts and starlings, the shuffling of a man

too thin to hope for lodging at your sign,

a random syllable, a charlatan—

that's me, a thread snipped out of the design.

If I could stroke your neck, sad pelican,

that curve of feathered flesh, that muscled line

might lift me out of this quotidian

unease. My hand that ambles like a vine

might touch the sea-swoop of your bony spine.

A DIALOGUE BETWEEN THE BODY AND SOUL

What but a Soul could have the wit

To build me up for Sin so fit?

So Architects do square and hew,

Green Trees that in the Forest grew.

—ANDREW MARVELL, "A Dialogue Between

the Soul and Body"

Body

I was too modest in those days.

I thought it took a soul to raise

a body up and warm its limbs,

the soul a forester who trims

and hews—yes, hacks down those like me

who greenly wait impassively.

But now researchers look in vain

for soul and find instead the brain,

that knot of cells that calculate

my chances for a meal or mate.

Soul

Granted, my jurisdiction's shrunk.

You walk without a household monk

to whisper canticles and threats.

Instead, your neurons place their bets

on curves of breast or biceps, tones

of voice, the drift of pheromones

across some real estate, a stash

of seed or mineral—some cash.

And guilt? The term's no longer in.

The neurons are immune to sin.

Body

Still superior, still the pose

of soulful intellect who *knows.*

We bodies don't pretend to solve

the mysteries. We just evolve

as best we can, breathing the air,

inching up the winding stair

to find our breakfast and our niche—

and progeny that make us rich.

Now where do *you* live, Mister Sky?

I've looked, I've called you. Did you die?

Soul

You're right, I've moved. I have a new

address, a neighborhood near you.

I've watched the motions of your eye

where careless scraps of bush and sky

are swept up by the retina,

electrified, and sent in a

neat bundle to the waiting lobe.

Your followers are right to probe

the subtle links in that design.

But look, the final turn is mine:

I catch the light scraps where they land,

weave them and work some sleight-of-hand,

anoint them, and—*voilà*—a world

where old perplexities are curled

like vines around a post, where song

comes clear and tides sometimes go wrong,

where faces wear their histories

and griefs take shelter in the trees.

MUSIC

Musick, the Mosaique of the Air

—ANDREW MARVELL, "Musick's Empire"

Cornet and cymbal, viol and the choir—

"Those practicing the Wind and those the Wire"—

all place their subtly colored chips of sound

just here and here until three vines have wound

their green chromatic stems around an urn,

a bunch of grapes, a bird. Where did they learn

to master this mosaic of the air?

Each marble quarter note is fingered there

where its clean edge will catch the echoing light.

Another motif now: the shadowed white

of fleece—six sheep—and Christ in golden stone,

seated, sandaled, lit by an overtone

of loss. A solo, a concluding strain,

and Christ is gone. Now scattered blue notes—rain?

No, larger cadences call in the sea

itself, and Neptune drives four sinewy

fish-tailed stallions through the drumming brine,

past dwarfs on dolphins, past the serpentine

border of eels, to our mosaic's slow

dissolve. We ride the water but we know

the surge that sweeps up dolphins and despair

is sound, not stone, a fragile twist of air

that sends its viney cipher to the ear

and then, like winter breath, must disappear.

The colors fade. An ordinary breeze

bends the long grass and shuffles through the trees.

SILENCE

Let moon be a metaphor

for what we leave

unsaid. All winter, we've been

clouded in, a rim of ice

sealing the house

at the eaves. But now

in April the sky lights up

behind the trees.

"Bright out tonight," we say,

sheets gleaming on the line,

the white gravel

curving away. A V of geese

honks north, still traveling,

thinking it's daylight.

Looking to the east, we see

the moon, appalling,

beautiful,

a mouth about to speak.

AUTHOR'S NOTE

The mosaics mentioned in "Music" are *Christ as the Good Shepherd* in the entrance hall of the mausoleum of Galla Placidia, Ravenna, AD 425–50, and the floor mosaic from the Baths of Neptune, Ostia, second century AD, with its dolphins, eels, horses with fish-tail bodies, nereids, tritons, and marine gods.

ACKNOWLEDGMENTS

Many thanks to the following journals in which some of these
poems have appeared:

Basalt

"Moon," "Music," and "Radiation"

Beloit Poetry Journal

"Cherry Pie," "Deaf Ear," "Path to the Cabin," and "Waning
Moon"

Chautauqua Literary Journal

"Oboe"

Driftwood

"Moustache" and "Negative Space"

Gettysburg Review

"A Bird," "Crete: The Diktaean Cave," and "Shepherd"

Hudson Review

"Christmas Night," "A Clutch of Mammals," "December 26,"
"A Dialogue between the Body and Soul," "Alarm Clock," and
"Poker"

MacGuffin

"After-Music," "Daughter in New York," "December 26" (pub-
lished as "Lake Effect" in an earlier version), "Midnight," and
"Open"

Poetry

"Christmas, Mexico" and "Wise Man" (titled "A Christmas Poem")

Poetry Northwest

"Script for a Cold Christmas"

Shenandoah

"Mario"

Snowy Egret

"Dust Mites" and "Scramble Competition Polygyny"

Third Coast

"Numbers"

"Exits," "The Fly," "Hippocampus," and "Silence" appeared in *Taking Notes on Nature's Wild Inventions,* a chapbook published by *Snowy Egret* in 1999. All of the poems in section 2 appeared in *The Fingernail of Luck,* a chapbook published by Mayapple Press in 2005.

Special thanks to friends who have read and helped to fix these poems: Dabney Stuart, Diane Seuss, Jane Hilberry, Ed and Brownie Galligan, and everyone in the Sunday group—Kit Almy, Marie Bahlke, Marion Boyer, Danna Ephland, Christine Horton, Gail Martin, and Susan Ramsey.